I0060749

Make Money Online Entrepreneur Series:

Book 6

Power of

Email Marketing

KIP PIPER

http://www.kippiperbooks.com

Copyright © 2014 by Kip Piper

All Rights Reserved

ISBN: 1886522-12-x
ISBN-13: 978-1-886522-12-1

YOUR FREE GIFT...

Want a free book?   Want access to more freebies and special offers through Amazon?

As a way of saying *thanks* for your purchase, I'm offering a free eBook that is only available to my customers.   Right now, you can get a copy of my book: *"28-Day Small Business Profit Plan: The Quick Start Guide for Business Success"*. This book is not sold anywhere else and can only be found on my website.

Plus, you will learn how to get instant notification whenever there is a new free book or special book bundles through Amazon.

Get the details at my website: **www.KipPiperBooks.com**

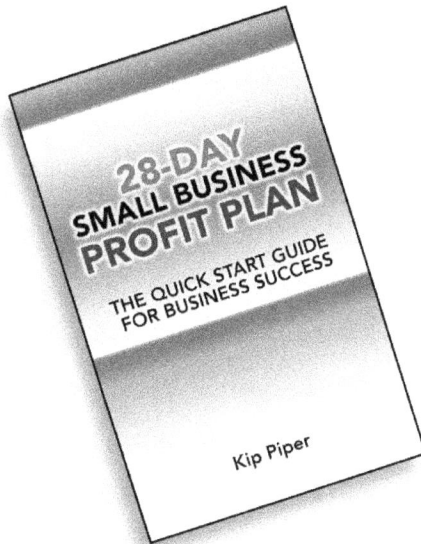

CONTENTS

AUTHOR'S NOTE

As you have probably experienced, the Internet and the websites on it are constantly changing. The information, examples, and screenshots presented in this book are accurate at the time of publication.

If you encounter any websites that have changed, please let me know by emailing me at: kip@kippiperbooks.com.

Remember, even though the website(s) may have changed, the principles, techniques and strategies in this book remain sound.

The links in this book are primarily affiliate links, which means if you purchase through the links, the price is the same to you and I receive a commission. This is the heart of affiliate marketing and entrepreneurship – which I am teaching you how to do with this book! I thank you in advance for using the affiliate links.

A FEW WORDS FROM KIP

Before I began teaching others how to blog and be successful with their online businesses, I wanted to be sure that I had something different to teach – strategies that are not easily found but can make a huge impact on success. The last thing I wanted to do is waste anyone's time. I wanted to offer something unique that would add both value and the potential for quick success for you.

Unknowingly, my research into online business success began in 1996 when I was first introduced to the concept of affiliate marketing. The potential for income excited me and I was quick to start experimenting with it. I joined Amazon.com and the few other affiliate programs available at the time. I added links on my website to products that related to my web design and Internet marketing business, with the purpose of offering quality resources to my website visitors and my clients. I encouraged and worked with my clients to include affiliate marketing in their overall online presence. I did this all in the hopes of adding to my income streams and eventually have affiliate marketing my dominant, if not sole, source of income.

But it did not come quickly, as others had promised or experienced. I totally, 100% believed in the concept of an online business and affiliate marketing (and still do), I understood the mechanics of setting up websites, creating products, and adding affiliate links, but I struggled with ranking my site high with the search engines and driving traffic to my site. Where were all the promised visitors who would buy what I offered or recommended so I could earn commissions?

Why were so many others achieving success? Why wasn't I experiencing the same success? Where was I going wrong?

I joined various mastermind groups. I purchased training programs from so-called "gurus". I bought books, read articles, watched videos, attended conference calls and webinars – I immersed myself in learning about blogging, affiliate marketing, and creating products.

The one most important thing I learned is that you need multiple websites, each focused on a different niche, to ensure a steady stream of income. "But," I asked, "if I can't get people to come to my first website, why should I spend more money and time creating websites that will not be visited either?" And each "guru" smiled nicely and said, "If you will upgrade your membership to our most expensive level, I'll tell you." But when I looked closely, I realized each "guru" was not living the life I wanted. In fact, most were working as hard or harder than I – with even less free time and income! They did not have the freedom of time and money that I wanted.

I didn't give up, though. I continued my search – knowing the one little "missing link" was out there.

One day I found it!

With this new knowledge, I knew without a doubt I could not only be personally successful with blogging, affiliate marketing and product creation, but now I could teach others those same strategies.

I realized that knowledge is what sets apart the training I offer – with this book and my other books which you can find at **http://www.kippiperbooks.com.**

This book is unique because it was written for *YOU.*

- YOU are someone who sees the potential in having an online business of affiliate marketing and product creation, but needs to know how to get started.
- YOU want practical strategies and advice that have already been tested and proven to work.
- YOU are ready for double-digit growth in sales.
- YOU are committed to following through with what you're about to learn.

This is why YOU are here.

Now please understand. Every piece of advice, strategy and practice has been tested on actual live blog, affiliate marketing and product websites – my own, my clients', and others. None of this is theory. You might then ask yourself, *ok, so how many blogs and affiliate websites has Kip done and what qualifies her as an "internet business expert"?* I think that's a great question. I wish more people questioned so called "experts" to see what qualifies them. As for me, I looked back on the last 15 years of stats and discovered that I have personally generated a 5-figure income in blogging, affiliate marketing and my own product sales – and that's just part-time!

If that's something you'd like to accomplish, you've selected the right book and series to begin with. I say "begin" because you'll soon discover that the learning process is a journey.

But don't worry! There's one more thing that qualifies me to lead you down this path – I'm just like you. It doesn't matter if you've never built a website or if you're already earning an income with blogging, affiliate marketing and your own product, and simply want to improve your sales. As you have already read, I've been wherever you are right now.

For anyone who reads this book and the entire *"Make Money Online Entrepreneur Series"*, and implements everything they learn, I can guarantee your business will move forward with more subscribers, sales and a stronger connection to your market. Like I said before, it doesn't matter if you've never built a website in your life or if you're already experienced, I've been there and can show you how to make blogging, affiliate marketing and product creation a successful income source.

But before we begin, I need you to do something. Connect with me on Facebook at:

http://www.facebook.com/TheRandomBlondeFanPage

I'd love to stay in touch and learn more about your journey.

You also are invited to check my website for more business books, and all of the books included in this *"Making Money Online Entrepreneur Series"*:

http://www.kippiperbooks.com

Thanks again for choosing to spend this time with me. Now let's get started!

"Done is better than Perfect!"

INTRODUCTION

This is Book 6 of the *"Make Money Online Entrepreneur Series": "Power of Email Marketing"*.

The entire series consists of more than 20 books, specifically written as an entire online business success training course.

Beginning in August 2013, I released one book a week, in the proper order to ensure success. If you follow the series from Book 1 to the end, one week per book, you will complete a 5+ month training course and master being an online entrepreneur! Of course, you can finish the series faster. Just make sure you fully complete the lessons in each book before moving on to the next. This way your success will be greater!

This series is carefully designed to give you every building block you need to build a successful online business. All of the guesswork is taken away, and by following this series, you will avoid most of the common mistakes made by new and even experienced online entrepreneurs. All is revealed – nothing is left out!

The beauty of this series is that you can pick up any book on whatever topic you need at this moment. Or you can purchase each book as it is released. Or ultimately, you can purchase the entire series in a bundle!

However you choose to use the information offered in this and the other books, you will be moving forward with intention and strategy for success in your business.

If at any time you have questions or desire personal one-on-one coaching for a particular topic, feel free to contact me at kip@kippiperbooks.com.

Here's to your online business success!

ONLINE BUSINESS SUCCESS CORE VALUES

Before we get started, it is important to understand, to be a successful online business entrepreneur, it is necessary that you stay focused on your business and have the core values that ensure that success. Here are the values that I have found to be essential to keeping focused and moving forward. These values will be at the beginning of every book of this *"Make Money Online Entrepreneur Series"*.

Be Passionate About Entrepreneurship

As it says, you need to be passionate about what you do and about being an entrepreneur. Being an entrepreneur will present the greatest challenges and the greatest joy you've ever experienced in the business world.

Commit 100% And GO FOR IT

One of the biggest things about being successful is being okay with putting yourself out there. Even if it's just a part-time business, commit 100% of yourself to the time you invest in your business. Commit to see it through and don't give up too soon. As the saying goes, "Don't give up before the miracle happens." Be patient and be persistent.

Build A Network of Support & influence

You must build a network of support and influence. This means building your Facebook community, building your Twitter community, and building your LinkedIn community. You must contribute to other people and help them be successful. By contributing to others and helping them be successful, you will become successful.

Get Comfortable with Being Uncomfortable

You're going to be doing a lot of things that you may or may not have done in the past. You can only grow when you're uncomfortable. When you're feeling comfortable and used to doing the things that you normally do, it's really difficult to grow, so you need to be comfortable with being uncomfortable see you can stretch and grow.

Consistent Growth & Improvement

It is important that you commit to consistent growth and improvement. We all need improvement especially if we are to grow and become successful, because staying up to date with the current tools and resources is essential. What helps you with consistent growth and continuing to improve is tracking your progress on irregular basis.

You also need to be okay with evaluating yourself and looking back at what you did and what you didn't do – without judgment. Simply observe and then recommit to the next step of growth and improvement.

80/20 Rule & Speed of Implementation

I'm sure you would've heard of the 80/20 rule (also known as Pareto's Rule) that 20% of what you do provides 80% of your success. So you need to understand that not everything you do is going to be perfect. Learn from it and move on. The quicker you get things done with the knowledge that you have, the more you'll be able to grow.

Flexible Persistence

Be persistent with everything that you do, and stay consistent with everything you do. The ones who experience the most success are the ones who are persistent in accomplishing their goals and are the most consistent in what they do. To be consistent, you must commit to regularly completing the tasks that ensure your success, whether those tasks occur daily, weekly, monthly, etc.

Surround Yourself With "A" Players

In business you deserve to surround yourself with the best and those who share your entrepreneurial spirit. You become like those you spend your time with. So choose carefully who you hang around with, so you are with those who think like you and make you stretch and reach higher.

The same goes for your employees. If you're going to outsource, you must select the best people who are competent and people you will enjoy working with. Avoid people who have negative attitudes. Surround yourself with those who embrace the concepts of small business success, entrepreneurship, and financial wealth.

Sell With Conviction

Be passionate about your product or service. Make sure you understand every aspect of it so that you can easily describe its features and benefits to your potential customers. If you have hesitations or doubts about your product, improve it so you don't have doubts.

Celebrate All Wins

Celebrate all victories! When you get that first sale, celebrate that first sale. Celebrate each new client. Celebrate each year of business success. Make sure you celebrate all wins. This is really important to maintain passion, momentum and to ensure success.

PICKING A MAIL SOLUTION

The first step to starting any email marketing campaign is choosing the right email marketing platform. This may vary depending upon where you are in your business, how complex you want to segment, etc., but I'm getting ahead of myself. Let's dive into how you can choose and make sure you are using the right email marketing platform for your business.

First, there are some questions you need to ask yourself when selecting an email marketing platform, a.k.a. an email marketing service provider.

1. Do you need to segment your list?

In other words do you need to take different pieces of your list, or steps/actions people will take, and divide your list based on those actions. This is called list segmentation – when you group segments of your list depending on actions they took, products they bought, webinars they watched, etc. How many different things you sell, or the type of product or service that you have, will govern how much you need to segment your list. It's important to keep in mind that some people try to segment too much. Keep it simple. More segmentation is not always best.

2. Are you going to need detailed analytics?

Different email service providers offer different levels of analytics, such as, open rates, click-through rates, unique click-throughs versus total click-throughs, etc.

3. Do you need a Shopping Cart?

More specifically, do you want your Shopping Cart to be part of your email marketing platform?

If your core business model is solely affiliate marketing, then you do not need a Shopping Cart. Why? Because you were going to be promoting other people's products and they are going to be processing the payments – not you.

If your core business model is information marketing, ideally you're going to want to have a Shopping Cart. If you're going to have a Shopping Cart and are going to process payments, then it's best to process them right through your email service provider.

Do you need to segment your list?

Segmenting your list is the act of dividing your list into smaller pieces to market different products and services two different "segments" or groups of people that are on your list. The reason you want to segment your list is that it allows you to more closely target to specific people. In other words, if you have multiple customer avatars and you want to put an upsell opportunity in front of only the people who have purchased Product A, or within the last 30 days, etc., segmentation simply allows you to divide your list based on actions certain people within your list have taken.

Businesses that are in different niches, or have multiple products, or offer a range of different affiliate products, need good segmentation. Conversely, the more simple is your business the less segmentation you need.

When you are starting out, you need much less segmentation; the more you grow, the amount you segment your list, and the amount you directly target those segments will grow along with you.

Are you going to need detailed analytics?

Let's now discuss detailed analytics and whether or not you're going to need them in your business. Email analytics are numbers that explain how effective your email campaign is. They include open rates, CTR (Click Through Rates), Bounces, Opt-outs, etc.

It's important to consider is the level of detail. For example, let's look at Bounces. There are different types of Bounces: Hard Bounces and Soft Bounces. A Hard Bounces is an example of an email account that simply does not exist. Hard Bounces indicate a faulty email address. A Soft Bounce means the email did bounce back and did not get delivered, but it's a valid email address. It may just mean that their email inbox is full so they cannot except anymore messages at that time. This is an example of how detailed you may sometimes need your analytics to be.

The more metrics you have, the more information you have to be able to I just and tweak your campaigns to make sure they are operating at full efficiency and maximizing the amount of dollars you are getting back for every single email that you send or sequence that you set up. I am a firm believer in having as many email metrics available as possible.

Do you need a Shopping Cart?

Shopping carts are a way to process orders online. Your customers can use their credit cards or PayPal to complete transactions.

If you plan on selling your own products as an information marketer, or you offer services as well, or you are a traditional business owner looking to process payments online, you're going to want to have your own shopping cart where you can process payments directly. If you are solely an affiliate marketer and not selling any of your own products or services, then you will not need a shopping cart.

I realize there are external shopping carts, but we are discussing email marketing in this book. Within email marketing, you should have your shopping cart within your CRM or email marketing platform if you're looking to incorporate a shopping cart into your business and collect online payments.

EMAIL MARKETING PLATFORMS

Now we are going to look at email marketing platforms. There are different levels of email marketing platforms depending on the services and features they offer.

Basic Email Marketing Platforms

IContact http://kippiperbooks.com/iContact and **Get Response** http://kippiperbooks.com/GetResponse are basic email marketing platforms and are an inexpensive way to get started. The downside is that they do not have that many features, such as, they do not offer a sophisticated level of list segmentation nor a shopping cart. The advantage is that they are an inexpensive and efficient to get started quickly. You can send out affiliate offers and other ways to make money online that do not require the more advanced features.

IContact and Get Response are good for simple email deliverability. You can make graphically appealing emails. IContact and Get Response are good providers in that their emails have a high rate of deliverability, which means your emails will get to your list —your content and your offers get in front of your subscribers.

IContact and Get Response are **not** detailed when it comes to analytics. They do **not** include a shopping cart, and they **don't** do automated list segmentation.

You can physically segment your list, but they do not allow for automatic segmentation based on action somebody took. In other words, if someone purchased a product, neither of these services would automatically drop them out of the "prospects" list/sequence into the "customers" list/sequence.

What IContact and Get Response do very well: they are very cost-effective by being inexpensive; they have good deliverability if you are building your list organically, so your list will get your emails.

Intermediate Email Marketing Platforms

The email marketing providers in this section are the next level of sophistication of functionality.

AWeber http://kippiperbooks.com/AWeber and **Constant Contact** http://kippiperbooks.com/ConstantContact are good, relatively inexpensive email marketing platforms. They have some additional functionalities over the Basic Email Marketing Platforms.

AWeber and Constant Contact are good at email deliverability, have more detailed analytics, and offer pretty good automatic list segmentation. These features are not the highest level but neither are they the lowest level. They are relatively simple to use as well.

AWeber and Constant Contact do **not** have a shopping cart. If you want to sell your own product, you're going to need a separate shopping cart.

As I have mentioned before, if you are going to sell your own product or service and you want to process payments online, having your shopping cart contained in your email marketing platform is a huge advantage. It allows you to segment your list based on money they spent, products they have bought, etc. AWeber and Constant Contact do **not** have this level of functionality.

Advanced Email Marketing Platforms

Now we're going to take a look at the Advanced Email Marketing Platforms which are much more comprehensive in the features and functionality that they offer. The biggest advantages to the Advanced Platforms over the Basic and Intermediate are access to a shopping cart and automated list segmentation.

Infusionsoft.
Small Business Sales & Marketing

1ShoppingCart®

InfusionSoft and 1ShoppingCart are pretty similar in that they both have shopping carts and high email deliverability rates. They also offer more detailed analytics and automated list segmentation.

1ShoppingCart http://kippiperbooks.com/1ShoppingCart has a fantastic shopping cart. One feature is a One Click Upsell. You can use this when a customer purchases one of your products and you can offer them the opportunity with one click to purchase another product at a higher price point. This is a huge feature when converting customers for greater income. Once you have a customer who has purchased, it is easier to get them to purchase more.

1ShoppingCart also has a pretty good autoresponder with detailed analytics. 1ShoppingCart does *not* do list segmentation very well. Because of this, 1ShoppingCart is significantly cheaper than the other advanced email marketing platform InfusionSoft.

InfusionSoft http://kippiperbooks.com/InfusionSoft really has everything. It has a fantastic shopping cart with one click upsell, detailed analytics, and a very sophisticated automated list segmentation functionality. It really is the most comprehensive email solution available.

If you are in information marketer, if you have a service-based business, this is an immensely powerful tool to grow your business. When you first get started, you won't use all of the features that InfusionSoft offers. But even if you use just a small portion of it and start setting up a lot of the automation features offered, it can powerfully change the way you do business.

In summary where that you choose a Basic, Intermediate or Advanced Email Marketing Platform, the most important thing is that you select a platform and *implement it*. Start building your list and sending out emails, whether you're sending out affiliate offers, or driving traffic to a webinar, or to sell your own products or services, you need to select a provider you feel is right for you at this time and for the next six months. Whichever one you choose needs to last you for a while because you don't want to have to then change to allow for more functionality or for marketing and selling your own product or service later.

If you plan on selling your products or services online, and you were going to market via email (which you will!), then I suggest choosing an email marketing platform that has a shopping cart, even if you don't plan on selling right now.

If you know you're only going to be an affiliate marketer, you don't need InfusionSoft or 1ShoppingCart.

So these are the things you have to consider when making your decision about an email marketing platform. I suggest that you do not make the decision on where you are right now, but instead make a decision based on where you want to be six or 12 months later, because you don't want to have to change email service providers as you start gaining momentum and as your business starts growing.

THE ANATOMY OF WRITING EMAILS

Now let's get into the nitty-gritty of email marketing – that's writing emails. In the following chapters we are going in depth into the structure and anatomy of an effective marketing email.

THE "FROM" LINE

It all starts with the "From" line, or who the customer or subscriber is seeing as from whom the email is coming.

The "From" line needs to be consistent, whether it's your email address and name or it's your company's name and email. That it be consistent is the most important thing, not how it is formatted.

However I will say that if the "From" line can come from you or some person in your organization, it is always best because it gives a personal touch.

When you are writing your "From" line, it's important to **not** change the "From" line from email to email so it looks like it's coming from someone different all the time. This will cause an increase in spam complaints. When you have an increase in spam complaints, this decreases your deliverability.

People on your list don't like seeing messages from people they don't know or they might not recognize, they might not even know it's from you. Typically this will also result in an increase in opt-outs. These are people that have chosen **not** to be on your list anymore. They do this by clicking the opt-out link at the bottom of your emails. This means you have lost your opportunity to market to them in other ways.

The reason this is important is because, if people are opting out of your list simply because you change the "From" line, that's a very amateur reason to lose people and lose customers.

As part of your business model, if you want to have multiple people sending out emails from your company, it's important that it's consistent. In other words, the first few emails you sent out should be from both of you. It is okay to brand of multiple people; the important thing is your customers understand and not be confused.

Changing or randomizing from whom your emails are coming is not a good idea. You want to be as consistent as you can in who you're sending emails from to your subscribers.

SUBJECT LINES

The next step to writing emails – even before you begin writing copy – is using the right "Subject" line.

"Subject" lines are extremely important. Why?

The "Subject" line is the first part of your email that your readers read. It doesn't matter how good is your content or offer if your readers don't open the email.

In other words, your "Subject" line determines on whether your readers open your email or not. If your readers don't open your email, they will never see your content or take the specific action that you are looking for them to take.

So when crafting your Subject line, it's all about getting your readers email.

What is a Good "Subject" Line?

Compelling

First, the Subject line needs to be compelling. It needs to compel your reader to open your email. The more compelling the Subject line the more emails that will be opened.

Examples:

- Boring Subject line: *How to lose weight*
- Exciting and compelling Subject line: *Stop dieting and drop 20 pounds in 30 days*

The second subject line is much more compelling and will cause your readers to be curious. This is something to remember: if you can create curiosity, you're always going to have a good Subject line. If you can create curiosity in your Subject line, you're always going to increase your open rates.

Controversial

Controversial Subject line can be good in getting your readers to open your emails, but can also turn off some of your readers.

You want to reserve Controversial Subject lines for very important emails, such as emails that contain sales content or drive your readers to webinars or to an affiliate link or some other purpose where you want your readers to take specific action and monetize the email.

Do **not** use Controversial Subject lines for emails that contain simply blog content or general information or industry updates.

Example:

- Good Controversial Subject line: *Everything you know about training your dog is WRONG*
- Bad Controversial Subject line: All of the other Gurus have been lying to you

A rule of thumb I try to follow in crafting my subject lines is to never put other people down.

With a good example above, your readers will resonate with this type of Subject line because, in my opinion, dog training at home is a topic that many people don't teach very well. There is a lot of information about it, but people have a hard time understanding and applying the information, and seeing tangible results.

With the bad Subject line, if you're positioning yourself as a guru to your list and you are putting down your fellow gurus, this will turn your list off to you. This put your subscribers in a negative psychology towards you and other people they associate as being similar to you, which will not lead to a higher level of results.

Ethical

No matter what style of Subject line you use, **all** of your Subject lines should be ethical and not untruthful, discriminatory, or misleading.

If you think it's possibly any of these, then most likely it is.

This is a very quick way to turn off a lot of your subscribers.

- Good ethical Subject line: *My students are killing it with this new*

strategy
- Bad/unethical Subject line: *Never work another day in your life*
- Bad/unethical Subject line: *Make 100K without lifting a finger*

Unethical Subject lines are not a good long-term strategy to get people to stay consistent with your messaging of your product. Even if you do end up selling a product that you have positioned unethically, such as, *Earn 100K in the stock market without doing anything*, it is not a sustainable approach simply because people will not have results unless they take some sort of action or have some sort of tangible strategy to follow to leave them down the path to success.

Merging Personal Information

The next element of crafting a Subject line that will really increase open rates is a technique common and email marketing – merging personal information.

Merging personal information into Subject lines, such as the first name or business name, adds a personal touch to your emails.

A lot of marketers do this in the copy, but if you can do this in the Subject line, it can greatly increase open rates.

To do this, you're going to want to look at your particular email marketing software's training on how to merge personal information into your Subject lines. Four instance, if you have your subscriber's first name, last name and email address, your email marketing provider can show you how to include each one of your subscribers' first names in the Subject line.

Measuring Good Email Subject Lines

It is actually very easy to measure good email Subject lines. A good email Subject line is going to be measured by using the "Open Rate" analytic inside of your email marketing software.

If all things were equal and we had two exactly the same emails and we had two segments of our list of 50 people each, but the only difference between the two emails was the Subject line, you can determine which is the better subject line by which one of these two segments of people have a higher Open Rate.

The Open Rate will always indicate the quality of a Subject line.

It's important to remember that every niche is going to have different Open Rates. Just keep testing different Subject lines, and keep monitoring and increasing your Open Rates.

For example, if you're going to send a one-time email, such as for a specific offer or promotion, first take a small group of your email list, divide it up, and test two or three Subject lines. You will see which Subject line has the highest Open Rate. You then use that Subject line for the email that you send out to your entire list.

Remember, when crafting your Subject lines, you want Subject lines that compel people to open your emails.

EMAIL BODY

The next step to effective email marketing is writing quality emails in the form of your Body content. The text or copy is the actual content of your email that your readers see once they open your email.

The Body of your email is the part of your email that converts your readers into visitors for your sales letters, your website, an affiliate offer, etc. The Body is the copy that is going to get your readers to take whatever action you're looking for them to take – typically to click a link to wherever you want them to go.

The first couple of lines of your Body are the most important. These lines draw in your readers and get them to read rest of the email.

Deliver Quality Content

When you were writing your emails, you always want to deliver quality Content. Delivering good Content is going to help keep your readers interested in what you have to say.

Not every email is going to be a sales content email. For example, you may write an email about a blog post you have just written, or perhaps about a video you just completed, etc., where you are providing content to your list but not a specific sales message.

Quality Content is important for every type of email, whether it is informational or whether it is for a specific sales purpose.

The strategy is, if you are giving your readers all of this great quality information for free, then they'll view and buy your products and services as having as good as and even better quality information. It helps build credibility.

When you write quality emails, whether they're just content emails or content around your sales copy, it will definitely lead to higher sales from your list.

Social Proof

It is always good to provide Social Proof – another important element of quality emails.

There are a couple of different ways you can include Social Proof in your emails. You can include testimonials in your emails, you can say how many people have already signed up for the webinar, you can direct readers to your social media networks, etc.

Social Proof is important because people like to do things that other people have already shown to do.

Build Scarcity

Scarcity is having only a limited number of units to sell, number of seats on the webinar, even scarcity in a timeline with a deadline to take action. Scarcity is always good when writing email copy. People naturally want to fit in and want what they can't have.

You want to write scarcity from the perspective of the action you want your readers to take. For example, if you're writing about a webinar, that webinar is airing at a specific time. You send out an email the day before saying there is less than 24 hours to take advantage of this opportunity to attend the webinar. After that, the webinar is going away and going away forever.

False scarcity is *not* a good idea. Only talked about scarcity if it's actually true.

Add Credibility

You always want to add credibility in your emails. Being a credible source of information is extremely important.

There are a couple of ways you can accomplish this. For instance, you can add credibility by having a **strong** social media presence. Another one is to consistently deliver good content.

Honestly, the easiest way to build credibility is to have confidence in your message. Most people lose their credibility simply by losing their posture and not retaining the fact that they *are* a credible source of information – not continually displaying that and having the confidence when writing their copy to continuously prove that to their list.

Understand that credibility does *not* mean you have to have been an expert for five years or 10 years. You can be credible by providing great information, by being a diligent student in the subject matter, etc.

A part of credibility is your posture and maintaining that confidence that you are a credible source throughout all of your emails.

Remember, while there are others that know more about your subject matter than you do, there are many who do not know was much as you, and to them *you* are the expert.

Overcome Objections

Remember, the email copy is what will compel your readers to take action – to click on a link to a sales offer, an affiliate offer, etc. If you can write quality emails and give your readers a solid call to action to click a link, the chances that your readers will purchase and become customers will be much higher.

An objection is a reason why a person may not buy. Overcoming objections in your email copy is a good practice. Any time you are able to overcome objections in your email copy, this is going to increase the chances of action from your readers, which will ultimately lead to more buyers.

Positioning of URL

The next important element to consider is the positioning of your link or your URL in your email.

In addition to writing good email copy, you want your readers to take a specific action. So the positioning of the URL or the link we want them to click is very important.

One link should be "above the fold" in your email. "Above the fold" simply means before your reader will have to scroll down to read the rest of your email. So you always will want to place your link relatively high up in the email. You don't want your first link to be your first line, but you definitely want to have it "above the fold".

There should always be at least 2-3 links in any email that you write. With every link it is important to have a call to action. Don't simply add a link and hope people will click. You have to have a call to action telling people to click the link to see whatever it is you are sending them to.

HTML vs. Text Emails

HTML emails tend to look better, if the user's email software is set to view HTML emails. Plain text emails don't look as good but usually convert better. Why? Plain text emails typically are simpler.

What is the difference between a plain text and an HTML email? It's pretty much just one thing. HTML emails can include images, graphic headers, stylized text with colors, different sizes and treatments with in the email itself. Plain text emails are just that – plain text – with simple links.

An important thing to remember, before you go out and spend time or money designing a fancy HTML email, sometimes plain text emails a better because they are simpler and the readers do not have all the other distractions. As a result, the readers are more apt to read the text and follow the links – and that's what we want!

Measuring the Effectiveness of Your Email's Body

Measuring the effectiveness of your emails body content is simply with the CTR or Click Through Rate.

The Click Through Rate is determined by taking the number of times your link was clicked and dividing that number into the number of emails that were opened.

$$CTR\% = Clicks/Opensx100$$

An important aspect of the Click Through Rate is the number of unique opens and unique clicks. Depending on your email service provider, they may or may not provide you with this analytic.

Some email service providers will calculate the Click Through Rate on the number of emails sent, but I prefer to calculate only on the number of opened emails. This is a much better metric because it eliminates the possibility that a subject line isn't very good, and as we know, a bad subject line will reduce the number of opens and subsequent clicks.

CALL TO ACTION

The next important element of writing effective emails is having an effective Call to Action. Some people may argue that your Call to Action is *the* most important piece of your email. If no one clicks on the links in your email, then your email was really pointless. So your Call to Action is very important.

A Call to Action is giving your email readers a direct action to take. For example:

- Just click <u>here</u> to learn all the secrets.
- Get free tickets to the event <u>here</u>.

Next are the elements of an effective Call to Action.

Clear and Direct

Be very clear and direct. I can't tell you how many emails I receive where the call to action is vague and unclear about what to look at, where to click, etc.

Make the actions your readers need to take clear and direct. If the message is vague, you'll have a much lower conversion/click through rate. Your Call to Action has a huge impact on your click through rate.

- Bad Call to Action: This is a link to learn more about the event <u>Event Details</u>
- Good Call to Action: To sign up for this free event click <u>here</u>

In the good example above, you are telling them **exactly** the action you want them to take – **exactly** what you want them to do.

Positioning of URL

We've already discussed this above, but want to reinforce the concept here.

One Call to Action should be "above the fold" in your email. "Above the fold" simply means before your reader will have to scroll down to read the rest of your email. So you always will want to place your Call to Action relatively high up in the email. You don't want your first Call to Action to be your first line, but you definitely want to have it "above the fold".

There should always be at least 2-3 Call to Actions in any email that you write. With every Call to Action it is important to have a link. Don't simply add a Call to Action and hope people will do what it says without a link to make it easy. You have to have a call to action telling people to click the link to see whatever it is you are sending them to.

Tracking Links

Whenever you have a Call to Action you want to be able to track how many people are clicking. So the different links that you have in your email should each have a different tracking link.

Remember, we always want to have at least two Calls to Action and two accompanying links. Just because we have two links in the email sending people to the same place, it's always good if we can separate those different links with different tracking links.

The reason for this is to test what positions in your email copy are getting clicked on the most. Then we know where we should be focusing our efforts for the best click through and conversion rates. The more we know about the metrics, the better we can adjust and tweak our emails. In other words, is everyone clicking on the first link, or are they completely ignoring it and really clicking on the second link?

You will need to check your email service providers software to determine how to set up tracking links.

Have Only One Offer or Specified Action Per Email

This is very important! When you are writing emails, you want to have only one offer or specified action per email.

I see so many emails that have, "Hey, click here for this offer!" and then some copy and then, "Oh, by the way, you can get this offer as well!"

You are going to have only one offer or specified action per email.

As mentioned earlier you will have multiple Calls to Action, but they are all to the same offer. So if you are writing an email asking someone to go watch a video, you were only going to send them to that one video. You *don't* want to be sending them to that video and then to something totally different, such as a blog post or an article or a different offer, further on in the same email.

You want to have a clear specified action and only one action or offer per email. But you can have multiple times that you mention that specified action within the same email.

THE SIGNATURE LINE

After writing the body copy of the email, what follows next is the Signature line. You may wonder why there is a whole chapter dedicated to the Signature line, but it is that important. The Signature line is a great opportunity for you to develop a connection with your audience – a voice with your audience.

Personable

This Signature line needs to be personable and reflect your personality. The "sign off" should be strong, like "To your success" or "To higher profits" or "To your health", etc. you want to avoid the more generic "Sincerely" or "Yours truly". It needs to be something more directly related to your offer, niche or voice.

If you are a success coach, then close with "To your success". If you were teaching your audience how to be profitable in a particular venture, then close with "To higher profits". If you're in the health and wellness niche, close with "To your health" or something similar.

This Signature line is a way for you to communicate and directly connect with your audience.

The Signature line does not have to be formal, either. You can close with humor. If you're talking about a funny blog post or funny video, you can integrate your signature with whatever humorous message you're sharing with your blog post for video.

Social Media Networks

Another thing you can do with your Signature line is build your social media presence. Your Signature can include links to your social media accounts. Typically social media links do *not* go to your personal accounts, but go to your business social media pages.

A guideline on whether to include links to your social media networks is, if it is a content email, then definitely include links to your social media networks. If it is a sales based email, if you are sending your readers to one of your sales pages or you are promoting an affiliate offer, you do not want to have any other links or distractions in your email. So do **not** include links to your social media networks in promotional or sales based emails.

Remember, when you're sending out a sales based email, you're one objective is to get them to click on the link to whatever you are promoting.

THE P.S.

Following the Signature line in your emails is the Post Script or P.S.

The Post Script is simply at the end of the letter or email, and is going to allow you to write something that you "forgot about" in the body.

Obviously, it's not something that you forgot about. The Post Script is a way to re-communicate or have another Call to Action in your email.

What To Include In Your Post Script

Call to Action

You should include a link with another call to action. Sometimes people won't read the whole email, and they'll just skim through it or scroll down to the bottom. They get to the, they're going to decide what the going to do. That's why in the Post Script it's nice to have a little bit of information to wrap it up and a direct call to action.

Tease the Next Email

In your Post Script, you can include a teaser about the next email you're going to be sending. When you're including teaser information in your postscript, this is really important only in pre-sale content emails.

For example, if you have a series of emails where you were potentially warming up the customer with content-based autoresponders, you always want to be leading to the next email. In other words, always be hinting that there is another one coming and your readers are not going to want to miss it.

This is only for pre-sale content emails. You'll never tease for the next email when you're sending out an email with a link to a sales page or an affiliate offer. Why? Because with a sales-based email, you want your readers to take an action now. All of your copy is going to be based on getting them to click the link to the offer.

However, in a content email, you should always be teasing the next email that's coming, because that will keep your readers interested in what you have to talk about and hopefully get them to pay attention to the next email you send out.

Examples:

Watch out for the next email where I'm going to be telling you about _____.

Be on the lookout tomorrow because I'm going to be sending you an email that's going to show you the exact strategy that I used to do _____.

CONTENT VS. SALES EMAILS

Here we're going to discuss the difference between Content and Sales emails.

When you use Content versus Sales copy will very depending your niche, your voice and your message, and how consistently you send out offers. For example, if you consistently just send out content emails, and then all of a sudden switch to all sales emails, frankly it's going to turn off a lot of subscribers and you're not going to see good results.

It's important to be consistent with the frequency that you send emails to your subscribers. Now with new subscribers you can set a different timing with them, but with your overall subscribers – people who have been on your list for a little while – it's important that you are relatively consistent in the way that you communicate with them. For example, if your frequency is every other day or once a week, you don't want to change it to every single day, and then change the frequency again to every third day, and so one.

If you only send out sales emails to your subscribers, you'll quickly get ignored. It's important that you have some sort of value add.

For example, let's say you are running a three-four email campaign and driving to a sale, you can have content around that sales campaign. So you can send out, for instance, two or three content emails around or pre-selling whatever offer you are promoting in the last email. That content can be based around the promotion. It's important that every email is **not** just "buy, buy, buy". Your customers will get turned off very quickly.

Another reason to include quality content is that you need to reaffirm your readers' decision to give you their email address.

This is where content kind of blends in with sales. Even in your sales-based emails, you can provide strategic content from which readers will get value, but it will also drive them to want to purchase the product of whatever you're trying to promote.

As for the frequency, how often you send the content only emails is completely up to you. What is important is any precedent you have set in the past. If you are new and just starting out, it's okay to send emails frequently. It's important that you stay consistent with whatever frequency you establish.

You also want to find a middle ground between the frequency Promotions and the frequency of Content. This is very important to maintain a good, credible relationship with your readers.

Many people are scared to send out sales emails. The truth is, however, if you only send out content emails and you try to get everybody to love you, your readers and subscribers are not used to you sending out sales emails, so they are more likely to be turned off when you begin. On the other hand, when you consistently include sales emails with your content emails, then your subscribers become used to seeing them and are more likely to click on the links and purchase what you were offering. While this may seem counterintuitive, this actually works.

The basic formula that I like to use and recommend is that you send two content emails for every one sales email. Depending on your list or your niche and its response rate to your emails, you may want to adjust this frequency formula to improve the response rate of your list.

SPAM

When discussing writing emails, it's important to mention spam, what it is, what it is not, and the Can-Spam Act.

First, do **not** get scared about spam. Spamming and the Can-Spam Act was set up to eliminate those people who are being deceptive – those people who are fraudulently acquiring lists, sending out bogus emails and trying to make money off of them.

Legitimate businesses were trying to generate interest and build value with their customers, promote products and services, are not the ones for whom the Can-Spam Act is meant to stop.

The Can-Spam Act is meant to stop those big, huge, fraudulent email senders and marketers. The online business you are creating and building through this *"Make Money Online Entrepreneur Series"* of books does **not** fall into that category.

It is difficult become an email spammer. Every email service provider allows you the ability to designate and report spam and block it from your inbox.

As an email marketer, just because you get "spam complaints", that does not mean that you are a spammer. As you send out more and more emails, without a doubt people are going to occasionally flag your emails as spam – and these are people who have opted into your list! It could be they're just having a bad day. It is nothing to worry about. Just understand that it's going to happen.

The Can-Spam Act is a law that sets the rules for commercial email, establishes requirements of commercial messaging, gives recipients the right to have you stop emailing them, and spells out tough penalties for violations.

How Do You Avoid Being a Spammer?

Don't use false or misleading header information.

- Header information is your "From", "To", "Reply To", and routing information – including the original domain name and email address. These must be accurate and identify the person or business who initiated the message.
- We all have received email from email addresses that don't exist or companies that don't exist or even from email addresses that don't belong to the sender.

Don't use deceptive subject lines.

- The subject lines must accurately reflect the content of the message.

Tell recipients where you're located.

- Your message must include your valid physical postal address.
- What makes this easy to not become spammers is that you want to do all the things that the Can-Spam Act requires. It's always good when you are trying to promote our products for other people's products that you come across as the legitimate expert, and one of the ways to do this is have a physical location and brand yourself as a legitimate company.
- Your location can be your current street address or a PO Box you registered with the US Postal Service. It can also be a private mailbox you registered with a commercial mail receiving agency established under Postal Service regulations, such as the UPS Store.

Now we are going to talk about how to manage your emails as they relate to the Can-Spam Act.

Tell your recipients how to opt out of receiving future emails from you.

- At the bottom of every email, you always have to include a way for your reader to opt out. This includes a clear, conspicuous explanation of how the recipient can opt out of getting emails from you in the future.

Honor opt out requests promptly.

- Most email service providers make it very easy for your subscribers to opt out of your list and they immediately and automatically remove the subscriber from the list. Why do email service providers make this so easy? Because they are more concerned than anybody about spam. If they have somebody who is using their service sending out spam messages, it affects their deliverability. One of the most important features about the email service provider is its deliverability. They have to be able to get your emails delivered to your list.
- Any opt-out mechanism you offer must be able to process opt-out requests for at least 30 days after you send your email message.

Monitor what others are doing on your behalf.

- If you hire someone else to do your email marketing for you, it really doesn't matter. The law makes it clear that, even if you hire another company to handle your email marketing, you are still the responsible party as to content, spamming, opt outs, etc.

Remember, the Can-Spam Act and spam really applies to spammers. As legitimate marketers and legitimate business owners putting out our own products, promotions and affiliate offers, the Can-Spam Act really does not apply to us.

THE BASICS OF BUILDING A LIST

Now we are going to discuss the most important segment of email marketing – building a list. In this and the next couple of chapters, we're going to give an overview of email list building.

What Is List Building?

List Building is the exchange of "valuable information" for email addresses you can market to in the future. The "valuable information" can be in the form of an e-book, video, webinar, or other free product.

Why Build a List?

Building a list allows you to do a variety of things, such as:
- It reduces the number of users who come to your website once and do not come back.
- It allows you to capture the names and emails of your website visitors.
- It allows you to consistently market to your subscribers and drive them to where ever you want.
- It gives you the opportunity to interact with your subscribers at any time on your terms.

Understanding the Reach and Speed of Emails

- Email travels almost instantly. With the click of a button, we can send an email and communicate with our entire list almost instantaneously.

- Email was the first form of media that you can directly deliver to any number of subscribers.

As an Internet marketer and someone who is looking to drive traffic and generate sales online, by far the most profitable to accomplish this is email marketing. That is why we are going to focus on this in the next couple of chapters.

THE ELEMENTS TO BUILDING A LIST

These are the components to building a list that we have to have in place.

Traffic

Obviously, without traffic – without people visiting your website – you have no ability to generate a list or capture their name and email address. Traffic is simply visitors going to your website.

Traffic sources

- There are a lot of different traffic sources. As an effective Internet marketer in generating traffic and income online, you want to try to leverage as many different traffic sources as possible. Why? Because some people are going to come in from one source, others from another, and perhaps others from a third method. So the better you can become at capturing traffic, and capturing and names and emails, and build a list from all of these different sources, the more powerful an Internet marketer you will be and the bigger your business will be.

Here are some common traffic sources:

- PPC or Pay Per Click
  - o This can be Facebook PPC, Google PPC, etc. Basically paying every time someone clicks on your link in your paid ad and goes to your website.

- Organic
  - This is when you have websites that are ranked high within Google and other search engines. The visitor clicks on the link to your website, completes an online form, and is added to your list.
- Social Media (Facebook, Twitter, LinkedIn, etc.)
  - Social media is a free source of traffic. You can take people from your Facebook personal profiles or business pages, or Twitter account, or LinkedIn profile, etc., and then drive that traffic to specific webpages where you can then capture and build your list.
- Offline Methods (i.e., Direct Mail)
  - Many people do not consider offline methods, such as direct mail and other lists that readily available to you. You can drive them to a webpage to generate traffic to build a list.
- Affiliate Promotions
  - Many people do not think of affiliate promotions as an effective way to build a list, but it's actually the quickest, easiest and cheapest way to build a list. If you can get an affiliate to promote your product or service, and drive them to an opt-in or sales page, when the visitor fills up that web form, you capture their contact information.

There are other ways as well. The list about is just some of them. The important thing to remember is it's all about traffic – it's the first step to building a list. Without traffic, it's impossible to capture any sort of information.

Email Marketing Software

Email marketing software allows you to send emails, hold contacts in a database, and manage those contacts. When we talk about email marketing providers and software, we tend to focus on metrics, deliverability, etc.

At its heart, email marketing software is simply a database. It's a CRM (Customer Relationship Manager) database and you need to think of it as such. The email marketing software and all of your contacts listed within is a database. That database is your money. The value of your Internet business is in your list.

Email marketing software also allows you to create web forms, follow-up sequences, tracking links, etc.

The Opt-In Form

The Opt-In Form is generated from your email marketing platform. This way when someone completes the form and opts-in to your list, your email service provider automatically adds that contact to your list.

Your Opt-In Form should always have a free offer to entice your visitors to opt in.

You need to go to your email service providers training to learn how to properly create and apply the code for your Opt-In Form.

A Website That Hosts the Opt-In Form

This website can be a blog, main site, mini site, squeeze page, etc. Remember, you don't want to have the web form on just one of these, you want to have the web form on as many different sites as possible and bring all of these different elements into your strategy of building a list.

There should always be a Call to Action on every single website where you have a web form to push your visitors to opt in.

Many people just put up a single web form and expect visitors to fill it out. This simply doesn't work. You need to have a strong Call to Action to incentivize and entice people to opt in to your list.

Thank You Page / Redirect

You always want to have a thank you page or redirect. It is very important to have one of these when people opt in to your list.

After the visitor fills out the web form, you can have it redirect to another webpage. On that webpage you can have a thank you message, an offer to one of your products, or an affiliate product.

This has simply been an overview of the elements to building a list so you can understand the basic concepts. The important thing to remember is that you want as many web forms and as many opportunities as possible for people to opt in to your list. The more opportunities you have and the more places you can be where people can opt into your list the better.

SIMPLE LIST SEGMENTATION

Earlier in this book we discussed email service providers, one of the important features of an email service provider is list segmentation. In this chapter were going to discuss some simple elements of list segmentation.

Why Segment Your List?

Segmenting your list allows you to market to different parts of your list. Why do you want to do that? It allows you to run different businesses to the same email marketing software account. It also allows you to offer different promotions to different people based on different actions they have taken.

For instance, you can segment out your buyers so they're not seeing offers to something they've already purchased. In addition, you can put other offers in front of them for products that they could potentially purchase based on prior buying activity, interests, etc. This is one of the most important reasons for list segmentation.

Separating your buyers from your prospects is the first place you should begin with list segmentation.

Remember to keep your list segmentation simple and not overcomplicated. If your segmentation is complicated, it just makes things more difficult for you and you really don't end up getting the results you want for the effort you put into the segmentation.

How to Segment Your List

How you segment your list really depends on the email marketing platform that you choose. The different platforms allow for varying degrees of segmentation.

Typically where list segmentation varies depends on the degree of automation of the segmentation. In other words, the more advanced and the more detailed the segmentation offered by email service provider corresponds to automated their process is.

As an example, say you have a list of 100 subscribers, and 10 of the subscribers are buyers. You can easily cross-reference the buyers to your list and manually segment them. Where segmentation becomes a benefit in your email marketing platform is, when someone buys or takes an action, the email marketing software will automatically remove them from different campaigns.

You want to look at your email marketing platform and how it segments your list. Remember to keep your segmentation simple. The important thing is to get promotions out there and worry about segmentation later.

Best Segmentation Practices

- Don't send the same offer to someone who has already bought that particular product.
    - o This is the easiest way to upset a customer. The most important segment of your list is your buyers/customers. The people who have already purchased something from you are the people you care about the most. They are the ones who will most likely buy from you again in the future.
    - o Don't worry about segmenting the people who have not bought from you. Why? Because they may never buy from you, so segmenting prospects can be a waste of your time.
- Make sure that if you have a bunch of different funnels that the same email address isn't in different sequences at the same time.
    - o You don't want to send to a prospect one offer in the morning and then in the afternoon send that same prospect an entirely different offer.

EMAIL BLASTS

This chapter is an overview of Email Blasts. An Email Blast is simply a one time or one-off email. It is not an email that is part of an autoresponder sequence or campaign.

An Email Blast can be a content only or a sales email.

Make sure that you don't have an email with a follow-up sequence that is going to "kick off" at the same time you're sending an Email Blast. In other words, if you have people in a sequence, you want to make sure that you were not sending them the Email Blast unless it makes sense in relation to the sequence.

Why Do Email Blasts?

Here are a few reasons why you may want to do an Email Blast:

- If you are promoting a new affiliate offer that your list is not yet seen.
- If you were promoting a time-sensitive affiliate, like a product launch.
- If you have a new piece of valuable content, such as a new blog post.

An Email Blast is one that you send out manually. It is not part of an automated sequence or campaign.

How To Do an Email Blast

The actual mechanics is going to be different from one email marketing software to the next.

You might have to create an email template.

You might want to choose what segment of your list you want to send it to. Or you can send your Email Blast out to your entire list.

Sending out an Email Blast is relatively simple and will depend on how your email marketing software is configured.

Email Blast vs. Follow-Up Sequence

The differences between an Email Blast and a Follow-Up Sequence are:

- An Email Blast is manually sent out from within your email service provider.
    - o You manually go into your email service provider, compose the email, then with the click of a button, send it either to a segment of your list or to your entire list.
- A Follow-Up Sequence is a pre-defined series of emails automatically sent based upon a subscriber's or customer's actions.
    - o A Follow-Up Sequence can be activated when someone buys – a series of emails automatically sent out based on their buying action.
    - o A Follow-Up Sequence can be activated when someone opts in – a series of emails automatically sent out based on their opt in action.

TRACKING EMAIL BLASTS

In this chapter we're going to discuss tracking the emails themselves and the metrics to look at every time you send out an Email Blast.

Should you be overly concerned about every one of the metrics listed below? Not really. What you want to look at is the difference in the overall metrics from email to email to see if there's a change in the pattern of your subscribers actions. As you send out more and more emails, you will realize that your numbers and metrics will be pretty similar based on your list and your niche. It's the change in the overall metrics in which you want to focus.

So let's now look at each of the metrics that you want to monitor.

Number of Emails Sent

This is simply the total number of email addresses that you sent your email to. You should know this number before you hit the "Send" button.

Number of Emails Delivered

This is how many emails actually got to your subscribers. Delivered Emails typically are numbers slightly less than the Number Sent. Your deliverability will probably never be 100%, especially as your list grows. However, it should be as high as possible, such as, 98%, 99%, etc.

Number of Emails Opened / Open Rate

This is a number of your emails that were opened from the emails that were delivered. Open rates can be increased by writing compelling headlines that get your subscribers to open your emails.

This is one of the places where you want to monitor the difference from email to email. If you send out an email that has an open rate of 40%. *(By the way, 40% is a very high open rate, so don't expect that. This is for example purposes only.)* And then you send out an email a week later that has an open rate of 7%. With a difference that extreme, you have to figure out what went wrong in the second email and why more were not opened.

Something else that can impact your open rate is the time of day when you sent your emails. Typically I like to send my emails in the morning. Most people tend to open and check email early in their day.

As your company grows and your list grows, it can be difficult to determine the best time to send out your emails. You don't want to get obsessive about time. If you can send your emails out in the morning to the largest segment of your list, that's always best.

All things considered, overall, open rates are more affected by the Subject line of your email.

Clicked, CTR (Click Through Rate)

The Click Through Rate is most commonly found by dividing the number of unique clicks into the number of emails that were opened, multiplied by 100.

CTR%=Clicks/Opens X 100

You can increase your CTR by writing more compelling email copy and/or changing your "Calls to Action".

Number of Spam Complaints

The number of spam complaints is simply the number of times people are clicking the "Spam" button in their email viewer. Remember, don't take these to heart. 90% of the time, the person who clicked this button is having a bad day and doesn't think your email was actually spam.

Again, you want to look at the overall difference in spam complaints. If you have a subscriber list of 1000 people and you get one or two spam complaints on average, then you send out an email to your list and get 15 spam complaints, that's when you need to consider why there was an increase in the spam complaints.

Number of Opt Outs

The number of Opt Outs is very important. For your subscribers to opt out, they must click on the link at the bottom of your emails.

Opt Outs are going to happen, but you can reduce the number of Opt Outs by delivering good content and not sending too many emails. In other words, if you start seeing the number of opt outs starting to increase, you need to ask yourself, "Am I writing good copy or am I just sending too many emails?"

Sometimes Opt Outs can happen when you're sending out certain types of promotions, such as affiliate offers or other product offerings. You really want to monitor your Opt Outs in this case because you don't want to turn off your subscribers because of the type of affiliate offers you are sending out.

Remember, if it's a relatively low number and it's consistent with what you see on a regular basis, then there is no need to concern yourself. But if you're testing a new affiliate offer, always check to see if your opt out rates increase.

Bounces – Hard and Soft

There are two types of bounces: Hard and Soft.

Hard bounces are the ones you should be more concerned about. Hard bounces are emails that don't forget to email inboxes because the email addresses do not exist. Honestly, some people that opt in to your list or other email addresses that you acquire will be fake email addresses. It's just going to happen.

What's important is that your hard to bounced emails are removed from your email list. You do not want to send to hard bounces. Some email service providers will automatically remove hard bounces, but if they don't, every week or so you want to pull those hard bounces out of your email list. Hard bounces will affect your deliverability.

Soft bounces, on the other hand, are a little bit different. Soft bounces are emails that don't get delivered, usually because the subscribers' email inboxes are too full.

You do **not** want to remove soft bounces. If someone has a soft bounce, typically because their box is too full, the chances are they aren't getting any other emails either.

So if it's a legitimate email address and it's a soft bounce, you don't want to immediately remove them from your list. Why? Because they will probably clear out some of the emails and they will continue to receive emails from you.

If you find that a series of soft bounces have occurred over a period of months, then you're going to want to remove them.

This is not something to pay attention to all the time, but every once in a while you might want to go through your list to see if you have a large number of bounces and start cleaning them up and segmenting them out as it will affect deliverability.

BONUS MATERIALS

Below is the link to this book's bonus material. I have developed this tools from my own experience as well as compiled from tools I have used from various training courses I have taken.

The mind map is built in XMind software. You can download a free version of XMind from **http://www.xmind.net**

The item is also available as a PDF.

Strategic_Plan_Email_Marketing.xmind
http://www.kippiperbooks.com/make-money-online/book06/Strategic_Plan_Email_Marketing.xmind

Strategic_Plan_Email_Marketing.pdf
http://www.kippiperbooks.com/make-money-online/book06/Strategic_Plan_Email_Marketing.pdf

MORE KINDLE BOOKS BY KIP PIPER

Ultimate Affiliate Marketing with Blogging Quick Start Guide
http://www.kippiperbooks.com/UltimateGuide

Make Money Online Entrepreneur Series:

Below are just a few of the books in this series. To browse the entire series, go to:
http://www.kippiperbooks.com/makemoneyonlineseries

Book 1 – Freeing Up Your Time – VA's, Outsourcing & Goal Setting
http://www.kippiperbooks.com/book1
Book 2 – Your Core Business, Niche & Competitors
http://www.kippiperbooks.com/book2
Book 3 – Blogs & Emails: Your Link with Your Customers
http://www.kippiperbooks.com/book3
Book 4 – Affiliate Marketing 101
http://www.kippiperbooks.com/book4
Book 5 - Driving Traffic with Organic SEO
http://www.kippiperbooks.com/book5
Book 6 – Power of Email Marketing
http://www.kippiperbooks.com/book6
Book 7 – Quick Income Formula with Advanced Affiliate Marketing
http://www.kippiperbooks.com/book7
Book 8 – List Building with Facebook
http://www.kippiperbooks.com/book8
Book 9 – List Building with Twitter
http://www.kippiperbooks.com/book9
Book 10 - List Building with LinkedIn
http://www.kippiperbooks.com/book10

ONE LAST THING…

As you can probably tell from my writing, my intention is to inspire and support more people to build a better financial future. It's a tough economy today, and I think personal growth in the field of small business is more important than ever before. Even though I have well over 20 years of experience as a successful small business owner and online entrepreneur, I don't have all the answers. In fact I'm still learning myself, I just have my own opinions, experiences and a passion for being my own boss to guide me through life.

Thank you purchasing my eBook and for taking the time to read it. I hope you enjoyed it and found value within its pages.

If you did I would really appreciate your support by taking the time to write a review for me on Amazon. Reviews really help the authors you enjoy to get noticed in a crowded marketplace, and it would allow me to continue writing the books for this series and other business books.

Please visit the URL below to let me know your thoughts:

http://kippiperbooks.com/book6

All of my books are offered completely FREE on the launch and I want to reward loyal readers by offering my new books to them FREE of charge when they are released.

So please visit my website KipPiperBooks.com and either download your free copy of "28-Day Small Business Profit Plan: The Quick Start Guide to Business Success" or just sign up to my newsletter in order to be kept informed when the next release is due. I hate spam, so I promise I won't share your information with anyone – not for love nor money!

Good luck! I wish you every success in your personal and business endeavors.

www.ingramcontent.com/pod-product-compliance
Lightning Source LLC
Chambersburg PA
CBHW070827210326
41520CB00011B/2141